D1062330

ST. MARGARET LIBRARY
BEL AIR, MD

ST. MARGARET LIBRARY
BEL AIR, MD

On the Front Lines

The Green Berets at War

356.1
GRE

by Michael and Gladys Green

Consultant:
Walter Sokalski Jr.
Deputy Public Affairs Officer
U.S. Army Special Operations Command
Fort Bragg, North Carolina

CAPSTONE
HIGH-INTEREST
BOOKS

an imprint of Capstone Press
Mankato, Minnesota

ST. MARGARET LIBRARY
BEL AIR, MD

Capstone High-Interest Books are published by Capstone Press
151 Good Counsel Drive, P.O. Box 669, Mankato, Minnesota 56002
http://www.capstone-press.com

Copyright © 2004 by Capstone Press. All rights reserved.
No part of this publication may be reproduced in whole or in part, or stored in a
retrieval system, or transmitted in any form or by any means, electronic,
mechanical, photocopying, recording, or otherwise, without written permission
of the publisher.
For information regarding permission, write to Capstone Press,
151 Good Counsel Drive, P.O. Box 669, Dept. R, Mankato, Minnesota 56002.
Printed in the United States of America

Library of Congress Cataloging-in-Publication Data
Green, Michael, 1952–
    The Green Berets at war / by Michael and Gladys Green.
    p. cm.—(On the front lines)
    Contents: U.S. Army Green Berets—Green Beret history—Recent
conflicts—Green Berets today.
    Includes bibliographical references and index.
    ISBN 0-7368-2156-2 (hardcover)
    1. United States. Army. Special Forces—Juvenile literature. [1.
United States. Army. Special Forces. 2. Special forces (Military
science)] I. Green, Gladys, 1954– II. Title.
UA34.S64G73497 2004
356'.167'0973—dc21   2002154769

Summary: Provides an overview of the U.S. Army Special Forces Green Berets,
including missions, members, history, recent conflicts , and modern equipment.

Editorial Credits
James Anderson, editor; Steve Christensen, series designer; Jason Knudson, book
    designer; Jo Miller, photo researcher; Karen Risch, product planning editor

Photo Credits
AP/Wide World Photos, 29; Bullit Marquez, cover; Lauren Rebours, 16; Wally
    Santana, 20
Corbis/Bettman, 12; Leif Skoogfors, 6, 8, 10; Sygma/Laffont Jean Pierre, 24, 26
Defense Visual Information Center, 14, 15, 19
U.S. Army photo by Cpl. Kyle Cosner, USASOC, 23
U.S. Army photo by Sgt. 1st Class Paul Avallone, 4

1 2 3 4 5 6 08 07 06 05 04 03

Table of Contents

CHAPTER 1

Learn about:

- Special Forces

- A-Teams

- Missions

Special Forces were among the first U.S. troops in Afghanistan.

The Green Berets

On a cold day, U.S. Army Special Forces soldiers unload a helicopter. They stack their supplies on the rocky ground of northern Afghanistan. The soldiers are an A-Team of Green Berets from the 1st Battalion, 5th Special Forces Group (Airborne).

Weeks earlier, terrorists attacked New York and Washington, D.C. Since then, the team has prepared for this mission.

The team is 90 miles (145 kilometers) into enemy land. They carry 200-pound (91-kilogram) packs. Their mission is to find and train friendly Afghanistan troops. The soldiers will bring weapons for these troops. The Afghan troops will use the weapons to fight terrorists.

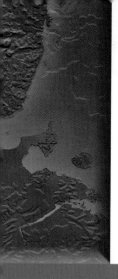

Who are the Green Berets?

The U.S. Army Special Forces are a force of about 10,000 soldiers. Throughout the years, they earned the nickname the "Green Berets." They are part of the U.S. Army. They serve in one of seven Special Forces (SF) units.

U.S. Army Special Forces train for four types of missions.

Each unit has 1,500 men. Congress does not allow women to be in the Army Special Forces.

The SF groups are divided into three groups of about 390 men. The headquarters for all SF is at Fort Bragg, North Carolina.

Each SFG(A) battalion is made up of about 130 men. The battalions are then divided into 12-man units. The small units are called Operation Detachment Alpha, or A-Teams.

A captain commands each A-Team. A warrant officer acts as second-in-command. The remaining 10 members of every A-Team are all sergeants.

Special Forces "Green Beret" Missions

At first, the main mission of the Green Berets was to train guerrilla forces behind enemy lines. A guerrilla force is a small group of fighters or soldiers. These groups often launch surprise attacks against a larger army. Today, the U.S. Army Special Forces have four main missions.

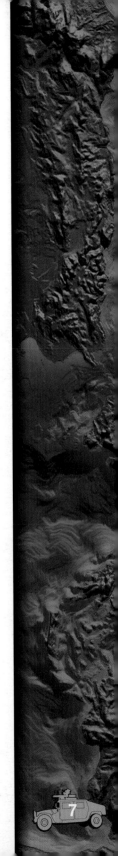

 8

The first of these missions is Special Reconnaissance (SR). During SR missions, A-Teams go behind enemy lines. They spy on enemy forces and report by radio. The A-Teams are careful not to be discovered by the enemy.

A-Teams also perform Direct Action (DA) missions. On these missions, Green Berets attack enemy troops and equipment. They may radio for support from Air Force planes or Navy ships.

In Combating Terrorism (CT) missions, Green Beret A-Teams study terrorist groups. The A-Teams find out where the terrorists are located. If a terrorist group has kidnapped U.S. citizens, the Green Berets try to rescue the hostages. Sometimes the A-Teams will attack members of a terrorist group.

For Foreign Internal Defense (FID) missions, SF personnel need to learn at least one foreign language. On FID missions, A-Teams travel to foreign countries. They teach foreign soldiers how to defend their countries. They also teach them things such as parachuting and how to fight in cities.

CHAPTER 2

Learn about:

- 10th SFG(A)

- Vietnam

- Operation Just Cause

Special Forces paint their faces before some missions.

The first SFG(A) unit was formed in 1952. This unit was called the 10th SFG(A). The reason it was named the 10th and not the 1st was to confuse enemies about how many SF units existed.

Southeast Asia Operations

In the mid-1950s, a guerrilla force was trying to overthrow the government of South Vietnam. Green Beret training teams arrived in South Vietnam in 1956. A year later, the 1st SFG(A) was formed.

In 1961, President John F. Kennedy saw a Green Beret military skills display. Kennedy was impressed. He ordered the Army to form more Green Beret groups.

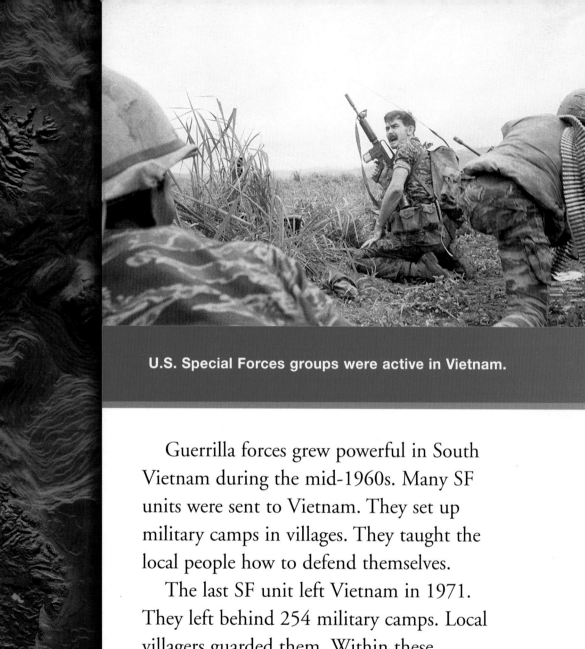

U.S. Special Forces groups were active in Vietnam.

Guerrilla forces grew powerful in South Vietnam during the mid-1960s. Many SF units were sent to Vietnam. They set up military camps in villages. They taught the local people how to defend themselves.

The last SF unit left Vietnam in 1971. They left behind 254 military camps. Local villagers guarded them. Within these camps, the Green Berets had built schools and hospitals.

Important Dates

1952—The 10th SFG(A) forms.

1956—Green Berets arrive in Vietnam.

1957—The 1st SFG(A) forms.

1961—President John F. Kennedy orders the Army to form more Green Beret units.

1971—The last Green Beret unit leaves Vietnam.

1989—Operation Just Cause takes place.

1991—Operation Desert Storm occurs.

1991—U.S. forces are involved in Operation Provide Comfort.

1994—Operation Uphold Democracy takes place.

1995—Operation Joint Endeavor occurs.

2001—Terrorists attack New York and Washington, D.C. on September 11. Green Berets land in Afghanistan.

2003—U.S. and Allied forces take part in Operation Iraqi Freedom.

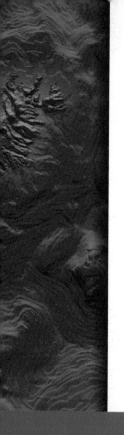

Latin American Operations

In the late 1960s, A-Teams carried out more than 400 missions. Most were in Latin America. Details of these missions remain a military secret.

SF A-Teams played a part in the invasion of the Central American country of Panama. A criminal group wanted to take over the government of Panama.

In 1989, the United States helped defend this government. The Army called the mission Operation Just Cause. U.S. forces defeated the criminal group's forces in heavy fighting.

Green Berets unload supplies from a plane during a mission in Central America.

U.S. Special Forces arrived in Panama in 1989.

CHAPTER 3

Learn about:

- **Green Berets in Kuwait**

- **Operation Provide Comfort**

- **Fight against terrorism**

U.S. troops celebrated with Kuwaiti people after Operation Desert Storm.

Recent Conflicts

In the early 1990s, soldiers from Iraq invaded the small neighboring country Kuwait. United States and Allied forces came to the aid of Kuwait.

On January 17, 1991, U.S. and Allied forces launched a large attack with hundreds of planes and missiles. The attack was aimed at Iraqi military targets in Kuwait and Iraq. The attack was part of Operation Desert Storm.

Operation Desert Storm

Before a ground attack could occur, Green Beret A-Teams went behind Iraqi lines. They checked the ground in different areas. Soil in the ground had to be strong enough to support the weight of U.S. and Allied tanks.

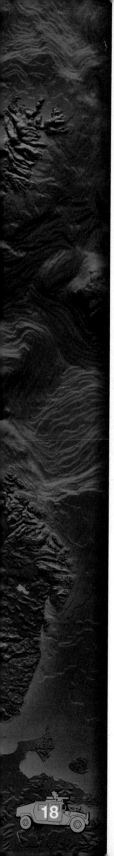

During Operation Desert Storm, an A-Team was attacked by 150 Iraqi troops. A gun battle broke out between the A-Team and Iraqi troops. The SF troops overtook more than 40 Iraqi soldiers. The SF soldiers used radios to call in U.S. fighter planes. The planes attacked the rest of the Iraqi troops. Green Beret units also helped to rescue U.S. and Allied pilots shot down behind enemy lines.

The Middle East, Haiti, and Europe

In April 1991, the 10th SFG(A) took part in Operation Provide Comfort. The mission helped more than 1 million Kurdish refugees in Iraq. The refugees were sick and starving. The Green Berets provided food and medical help.

During 1992 and 1993, the Army sent SF A-Teams to the country of Haiti. In 1994, they took part in Operation Uphold Democracy. A corrupt military group ruled Haiti. The people of Haiti did not want a military government. Green Berets made sure Haitians were allowed to vote for the leader they wanted.

Green Berets often train another country's soldiers.

Starting in 1995, Green Berets played an important peacekeeping role in southern Europe. The United States called these missions Operation Joint Endeavor. Much fighting had taken place in the area. People fought because of religious differences. With their language and military skills, SF teams helped restore order to the area.

U.S. Special Forces searched for terrorists during
Operation Enduring Freedom.

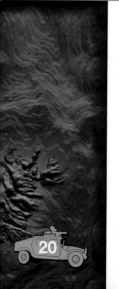

Operation Enduring Freedom

Terrorists from the Middle East attacked
New York and the Washington, D.C. area
on September 11, 2001. Thousands of
Americans and foreign visitors died because
of these attacks.

The terrorist group that planned the attacks was based in Afghanistan, a country in Central Asia. A group called the Taliban ruled Afghanistan. The United States asked the Taliban to turn over the leaders of the terrorist group. They refused. The U.S. government decided to prevent more terrorist attacks by invading Afghanistan.

American planes began to bomb the country on October 7, 2001. Twelve days later, the first SF A-Team arrived. They landed in Afghanistan by helicopter. Soon, 18 A-Teams were in Afghanistan.

The A-Teams quickly organized Afghan civilians. They trained them as guerrilla armies. The U.S. Air Force and Navy also took part in the training.

The Green Berets organized a force large enough to push the Taliban government from power. The last organized Taliban forces in Afghanistan surrendered on December 6, 2001. Green Berets continue to be involved in anti-terrorism action in Afghanistan and throughout the world.

Ground Mobility Vehicle

- **Function:** Armed Reconnaissance Vehicle
- **First Used:** 1985
- **Road Speed:** 65 miles (105 kilometers) per hour
- **Range:** 300 miles (483 kilometers)
- **Weight:** 6,087 pounds (2,761 kilograms)

The Green Berets' Ground Mobility Vehicle (GMV) is a modified version of the Army's standard High Mobility Multipurpose Wheeled Vehicle (HMMWV). It is a four-wheel drive vehicle that can drive on all types of surfaces. The civilian version of the Army's HMMWV is called a Hummer.

A diesel engine powers the large GMV. The GMV is 6 feet (1.8 meters) tall, and 15 feet (4.6 meters) long. It is seven feet (2.1 meters) wide. This wide stance makes the GMV stable. It is almost impossible to roll over.

Only a few Green Berets units use the GMV. Each GMV has a crew of three men. The crews are sent to special off-road training schools where they learn to drive GMVs in rugged areas.

ST. MARGARET LIBRARY
BEL AIR, MD

CHAPTER 4

Learn about:

- Q-Course

- SATCOM

- M4A1 carbine

Special Forces soldiers are trained to move quietly through water.

Today's Green Berets

Many U.S. leaders believe that the days of big armies are over. In future wars, a smaller number of troops will be sent into battle. Those who do go must be the best troops. The Army must select only the most skilled soldiers.

Training

The U.S. Army Special Forces have a tough admission policy. Soldiers must pass a series of tests during a 21-day period.

If a soldier passes, he moves to the Special Forces Qualification course, nicknamed the "Q Course." When a soldier passes this course, he receives his green beret to wear.

The soldier must then go to a language school. After he learns at least one foreign language, the soldier is fully qualified as a Special Forces soldier.

The best known uniform feature of the Army's Special Forces is the beret. Green berets were first worn by SF troops training in Europe in the 1950s. Soldiers bought the berets from civilian stores. Soldiers throughout the world soon wore the green berets.

Berets were popular in Europe. The U.S. Army's top generals did not like the American soldiers wearing berets. The generals thought the Special Forces should look like other American soldiers. The generals said the berets could not be worn. The Special Forces soldiers ignored the orders and wore the berets anyway.

President John F. Kennedy heard about the berets worn by the SF soldiers. He liked the idea. Kennedy believed that these troops performed tough missions. He thought they should be allowed to wear something that would set them apart from other Army soldiers.

The Army's generals heard that the president liked the berets. They quickly changed their minds. Since then, all Army Special Forces soldiers have worn berets. The original berets worn were green. Today, many Army members wear brown, maroon, or black berets.

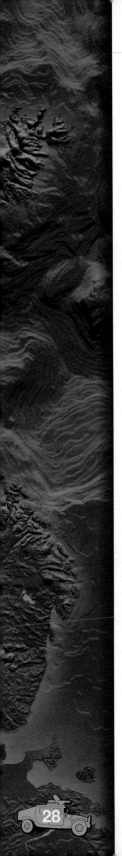

Communications

SF units are often assigned to missions that will take them into enemy territory. They must be able to stay in touch with each other and their commanders.

For long-range communications, SF units use a lightweight satellite system called SATCOM. With this system, they can talk to almost anybody in the world.

Weapons

The main weapon of the Green Beret soldiers is a M4A1 carbine. It carries 30 rounds of ammunition. It can fire one bullet at a time, or it can fire on full automatic mode. On this mode, many bullets are fired each time the trigger is pulled.

Green Beret units also carry the M249 Squad Automatic Weapon (SAW). The SAW can carry 200 rounds of ammunition. It can hit targets at a distance of 2,600 feet (800 meters).

Sniper rifles play an important role in many SF missions. Many A-Team snipers must hit targets 3,200 feet (1,000 meters) away. They use the M82A1 heavy sniper rifle. It carries five rounds of ammunition.

SF Forces are trained to use a M4A1 carbine.

Future of the Green Berets

Special training and equipment prepares
U.S. Special Forces for future conflicts.
Beginning in March 2003, U.S. Army Special
Forces soldiers entered Operation Iraqi
Freedom. U.S. and Allied forces operated
within the desert country of Iraq. Many Green
Beret missions in Iraq remain a military secret.

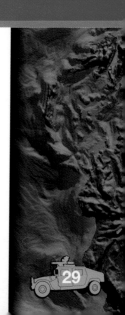

29

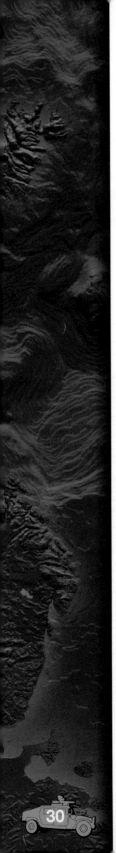

Words to Know

allies (AL-eyes)—people, groups, or countries that work together

guerrilla (guh-RIL-ah)—a member of a small group of fighters or soldiers; guerrilla forces often attack larger armies by surprise.

missile (MISS-uhl)—an explosive that can fly long distances

mission (MISH-uhn)—a military task

parachute (PA-rah-shoot)—a large piece of strong, lightweight fabric; parachutes allow soldiers to jump from airplanes safely to the ground.

personnel (purss-uh-NEL)—the people who work for the Army

To Learn More

Goldberg, Jan. *Green Berets: The U.S. Army Special Forces.* Inside Special Operations. New York: Rosen Publishing Group, 2002.

Green, Michael. *U.S. Army Special Operations.* Serving Your Country. Mankato, Minn.: Capstone Press, 2000.

Kennedy, Robert C. *Life in the Army Special Forces.* On Duty. New York: Children's Press, 2002.

Useful Addresses

U.S. Army Public Affairs
Office of the Chief of Public Affairs
1500 Army Pentagon
Washington, DC 20310-1500

U.S. Military History Institute
22 Ashburn Drive
Carlisle, PA 17013-5008

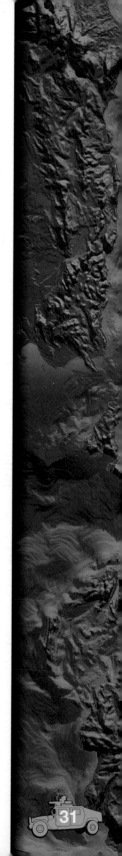

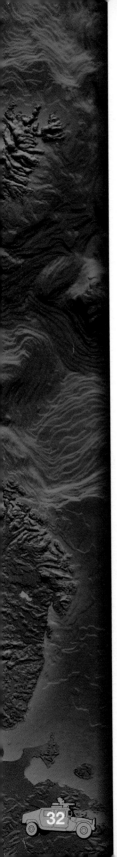

Internet Sites

Do you want to find out more about U.S. Army Green Berets? Let FactHound, our fact-finding hound dog, do the research for you.

Here's how:

1) Visit *http://www.facthound.com*
2) Type in the **Book ID** number: **0736821562**
3) Click on **FETCH IT**.

FactHound will fetch Internet sites picked by our editors just for you!

Index